Heaven Is For Real
The Book Isn't
An Astounding Refutation Of A Story
About A Trip To Heaven And Back

D. Eric Williams

For Ed Novak

· Contents ·

· One ·
The Story

In July of 2011 I was asked to read and critique the book *Heaven Is For Real,* written by Todd Burpo with Lynne Vincent. Although this is not the type of book I would normally read I agreed to do so, since the request was exigent (and I received the book free of charge).

In a nut shell, *Heaven Is For Real* concerns the "astounding story of [Colton Burpo's] trip to heaven and back." However, a cursory reading of the book uncovers a whole host of difficulties with that claim.

The book outlines the tale of Colton Burpo's emergency surgery for a ruptured appendix and the startling revelations that followed. In the months and years after the successful surgery Colton began to unfold a fantastic story to his parents. He first told them angels sang to him while he was in the hospital. Next he said he was in heaven with Jesus, sitting on his lap. While there, he saw his father praying in a small room at the hospital while his mother was in a different room praying and talking on the phone. Colton told his Mom and Dad he met John the Baptist in heaven, that Jesus Christ has a rainbow colored horse and wears a golden crown with a pink diamond.

According to the story, Colton was given "homework" to do while in heaven – apparently while he stayed at the home of his great-grandfather named Pop. We are told everyone in heaven has wings and everyone flies from place to place, except Jesus Christ, who goes up and down like an elevator. We are also informed everyone has a light above their head (which Mr. Burpo interprets as halos).

Colton also told his parents that God is "really, really big" so big he holds the entire world in his hands. He further informed his folks that Jesus sits at the right hand of God while Gabriel is at the left. Meanwhile, the Holy Spirit who is "kind of blue" sat somewhere in the vicinity as well. It is while Colton was supposedly sitting in this august assembly that someone came up to him and asked if he was the son of

Todd Burpo. This was Pop, Colton's great-grandfather. But rather than being an old man he looked to be around 30 years of age.

Colton also saw the gates of heaven, made of gold and pearls and after his trip to heaven he was "obsessed with rainbows" because of all the colors he saw there.

According to Mr. Burpo, Colton saw "power shot down from Heaven" by the Holy Spirit when his father was preaching (Mr. Burpo is the pastor of the Wesleyan Church in Imperial Nebraska). He also disclosed there are swords in heaven and that they will be used in the last battle – a battle that destroys the world and in which Todd Burpo participates. In this battle, the angels and adult male Saints fight against literal dragons and monsters while the women and children stand by to watch.

Moreover, Colton surprised his parents with the claim he met "a sister" in heaven – a child his mother had lost to a miscarriage some years before. His parents had never told him about the miscarriage and so they were shocked by his assertion, even while they found a measure of solace in being told the child (revealed as a girl) was in heaven - adopted by God himself.

Colton also says he saw Satan while he was in heaven but refused to describe his appearance and indeed he "went rigid, he grimaced, and his eyes narrowed to a squint" when asked to do so.

Finally, the entire visit – which seemed to last for days – took only three minutes. There is a bit more information about Colton's heavenly experience in the book but these particulars will suffice.

· Two ·
A Few Practical Problems

Probably the most obvious problem with the story is the fact that Colton told his tale over a period of years. It seems he came up with "heavenly tidbits" every now and again as his imagination moved him. Yet it is typical for a person to tell their entire tale as quickly as possible if they experience something as dramatic as Colton allegedly did. Mr. Burpo does not provide any explanation for Colton's failure to do so.

Throughout the book Mr. Burpo claims his son's innocence as evidence he really did go to heaven since it was after his stay in the hospital that Colton began to speak of things his father contends no four year old should understand.

However, Mr. Burpo tips his hand in the prologue when he tells us Colton had wanted the angels to sing "We Will Rock You" while he was undergoing surgery. Now, if Colton really did say this, it tells us that he was just like any other four-year-old boy who attended preschool and Sunday school and interacted with others in his community on a regular basis (for instance, "We Will Rock You" is standard fare at most high-school sporting events). In other words, Colton had absorbed far more information about the world than his father gives him credit for. After all, the gay pride anthem "We Will Rock You" is not on the play list of most evangelical Christian homes (or at least it shouldn't be) and I doubt the tune was heard on a regular basis in the Burpo household. The point is, Colton undoubt-edly accumulated plenty of information about life throughout his four years. Indeed, there is nothing Colton Burpo talked about in the months following his experience at the hospital that was somehow beyond his understanding.

This includes his claim he met his "other sister" in heaven. This aspect of Colton's alleged heavenly visit did not emerge until some months after the event. His parents say they had never told him about the miscarriage, although they had told his older sister. Now, it would require a certain amount of willful naivete to believe Colton had not heard about the loss of the baby prior to his statement about a sister in heaven. I have nine children and I can tell you, kids often pick up on things that daddy and mommy are certain they have kept under wraps. Indeed, it is not unlikely that Mr. and Mrs. Burpo specifically discussed the possibility of their baby being in heaven after Colton began to share his story. In any case, this claim of esoteric knowledge on the part of their son is entirely unconvincing. If it is true they had not told Colton about the miscarriage than I have no doubt he figured things out from what he overheard around the home or even at church. Indeed, it is typical for every tidbit of gossip that leaks out at church to soon become common knowledge, whispered about amongst parishioners, often right in front of the very people who shouldn't know.

Mr. Burpo also uses Colton's lack of knowledge concerning sashes as evidence his story is authentic. Once again, I find it impossible to believe a 10-year-old (the age at which Colton supposedly learned the definition of "sash") would be without this knowledge – especially a child raised in the church attending

Sunday school regularly, with Bible story books read to him each night.

The same can be said about the light above the heads of the people Colton saw in heaven. Mr Burpo claims his son would not have known about halos, yet there are plenty of child's Bible story books and other commonly available materials depicting saints and angels with auras. Ditto for the wings. It seems obvious that Colton's description of heaven originated in his own active imagination as fueled by his environment.

I suppose I could go on (knowing Jesus has a cousin, the wounds on "Jesus" body etc.) but my point is, none of the things that rocked Mr. Burpo to his core, sent him reeling, shocked him or blew his mind are particularly astounding. Indeed, it would require someone who has little familiarity with children - or people in general for that matter - to find these particular "proofs" so convincing. Indeed, the entire story (with one exception referenced below) is easily explained as the product of a normal childish imagination.

· Three ·
A Few Theological Problems

The claim of a heavenly visit followed by a disclosure of the journey is itself contrary to Scripture. The Apostle Paul *was caught up to paradise. He heard inexpressible things, things that man is not permitted to tell* (2 Corinthians 12:4) but this event was so unusual, even Paul was in danger of developing an arrogant attitude. Thus *to keep me from becoming conceited because of these surpassingly great revelations, there was given me a thorn in my flesh, a messenger of Satan, to torment me* (2 Corinthians 12:7). It is implausible to suggest God would change his mind about this and give the go ahead for a visit to heaven by a child less than four years old - and then approve the writing of a book to publicize the adventure. It is also interesting that Paul was not sure he had actually visited Paradise or if his experience was only a vision (2 Corinthians 12:1-4). Thus the biblical approach; recognize your inability to fathom such an occurrence and keep it to yourself!

The apostle John was likewise caught up to heaven but unlike Paul was commanded to write what he saw. However, what John relates is not literal but highly symbolic. In John's vision, Jesus Christ is pictured as a seven horned and seven eyed Lamb with his throat slashed (Revelation 4:6). The Christ is also pictured as *one like the Son of Man, clothed with a garment down to the feet and girded about the chest with a golden band. His head and hair were white like wool, as white as snow, and His eyes like a flame of fire; His feet were like fine brass, as if refined in a furnace, and His voice as the sound of many waters; He had in His right hand seven stars, out of His mouth went a sharp two-edged sword, and His countenance was like the sun shining in its strength* (Revelation 1:13-16). In addition John, *saw heaven opened, and behold, a white horse. And He who sat on him was called Faithful and True, and in righteousness He judges and makes war. His eyes were like a flame of fire, and on His head were many crowns. He had a name written that no one knew except Himself. He was clothed with a robe dipped in blood, and His name is called The Word of God* (Revelation 19:11-13). Clearly, John's account cannot be read literally. The entire book is emblematic, designed to convey literal truth through fantastic symbolism drawn from the Old Testament. In other words, John was not commissioned to provide an actual description of heaven but to tell about the unfolding of God's eternal plan in symbolic terms.

Nevertheless, Mr. Burpo's certitude concerning Colton's story rests upon a particular interpretation of The Revelation that is sharply at odds with a symbolic understanding of the text. Apparently, Mr. Burpo reads The Revelation literally. In other words, he believes the city described therein is literally heaven or is an actual heavenly city, truly made of gold, pearls, jewels and so on. However, if we interpret The Revelation as symbol (as indicated by the first verse of the book) then Mr. Burpo's entire narrative collapses like a house of cards..

For instance, on page 105 of the book, we are told Colton "saw the gates of heaven, he said: 'they were made of gold and there were pearls on them.' The heavenly city itself was made of something shiny, 'like gold or silver'." Mr. Burpo sees this as irrefutable proof his son was actually in heaven. Of course this assumes Revelation 21:9 and following should be understood as a literal description of heaven. Nonetheless, there are very few commentators who agree with Mr. Burpo on this. The text itself tells us that the angel showed John *the Holy City, Jerusalem, _coming down out of heaven from God_* (Revelation 21:10 underline added) not a Holy City *in* heaven. Therefore, most theologians understand this as a symbolic description of the church. For example, Henry Ironside says, "by this great city descending out of heaven from GOD, I understand then the diffusion of heavenly principles over all this earth during the Millennium by the heavenly saints, for it is through His saints that the Lord is going to claim His inheritance. We may learn in this symbolic description of the city, the great guiding principles which are to hold full sway in that coming age, and which are full of instruction for us at the present time."[1]

---

[1] Henry A "Harry" Ironside, *Ironside's public domain commentary texts*, Dr. David S. Thomason ed., e-Sword edition, (2011). Additional comments (in no particular order) concerning

A Few Theological Problems

Another obsession described in the book (page 115 etc.) is Mr. Burpo's search for an accurate depiction of Jesus. In the years following Colton's experience, his father made it a point to ask him if any of the pictures of Jesus they ran across were accurate characterizations. Over and over Colton would say the illustrations fell short. One day, Mr. Burpo found an image online of a painting by Akiane Kramarik, the child prodigy who at age eight painted a picture titled "The Prince Of Peace." Upon viewing the picture Colton declared "dad, that one's right." Mr. Burpo goes on to say, "knowing how many pictures Colton had rejected, Sonja and I finally

---

Revelation 21:9 from the resources I have at hand include: ...The pure and holy Christian Church, (Adam Clarke); ...represents the redeemed church now to be received into permanent union with its Lord, (Albert Barnes); ...[the angel is saying] I will show thee the whole church, (Matthew Poole); ...all the elect of God, (John Gill); ...the glorified church, (B. W. Johnson); The principle concern of this description is to show that the Christian church is the true fulfillment of the people Israel, (Earl Palmer); The Jerusalem that descends to earth from heaven is the church of the Lord Jesus Christ, (Simon J. Kistemaker); In beautiful symbol, the pattern of what the true Church of Christ, even now and here, should ever aspire to be. ...what we have here is the description of the true New Testament Church, (The Pulpit Commentary); The picture is not, of course, intended to evoke images of space stations, or of cities literally floating in the air; rather, it indicates the divine origin of "the city which has foundations, whose architect and builder is God" (Hebrews 11:10), (David Chilton)

felt that in Akiane's portrait, we'd seen the face of Jesus. Or at least a startling likeness" (page 142). However, there are some problems with this notion.

Akiane Kramarik began painting at age four at the prodding of a voice that came to her one day in a vision. Akiane says, "the earliest memory I can recall is when I was around four, four and one half years old, one day I started having these very amazing, mysterious visions, this voice was calling me and guiding me though these galaxies, and he, I asked him, you know, who are you, and I started calling him god."[2] Her experience is not unlike that of other psychics or spiritists. For instance Peter Hurkos, a psychic healer, says he began to paint pictures of his visions at the behest of "the voice." Indeed, "the voice not only gives information about the external world – past, present, and future – but also gives instruction in the arts. It sounds very much like the techniques used by the Soviet hypnotist Vladimir Raikov, who was able to 'reincarnate' great masters of painting in the minds of his subjects, thus producing competent artists in a few sessions. There is power here.

---

2 Found at http://www.youtube.com/watch?v=NKkBBDEc-4I& feature=related

Power to give information and power to direct and control personal development. That power is personal: being to being."[3]   Moreover, that power is clearly demonic.

In spite of her Orphic experiences, there are some who claim Akiane is a born-again Christian. But according to her own witness, "I have to tell you, we went through almost everything, from being Christian, to catholic, we studied Buddhism; at this particular point every single one of my siblings have their own path, I have my own, my parents have theirs, my brothers have theirs. I cannot say what they believe in or what path they are choosing, but I can say that for me, I'm the same person I was when I was four years old – I haven't changed and since nobody taught me who god was I found god myself and he's been there for me through the years ...so I don't belong to any denomination or religion, I just belong to god – I'm spiritual – I like that word. [Concerning their spiritual journey] it didn't change anybody because everyone was so supportive even before the transformation."[4]

---

3 Gary North, *Unholy Spirits: Occultism And New Age Humanism,* (Fort Worth: Dominion Press, 1986), 182 – 183.
4 See, http://www.youtube.com/watch?v=cYDzUTZys8g& feature =player_embedded#at=24

There is more. Although Akiane painted "The Prince Of Peace" in response to a vision, she required a model in order to complete the painting. She began to pray to her god and in response to her prayers she was a sent a very tall (Caucasian) carpenter who was going door to door looking for work. Upon being asked, he agreed to sit for the portrait. Thus, Mr. and Mrs. Burpo did not see the face of Jesus but the face of a man living in Idaho, painted by a demonically inspired young girl. In addition, if this is the face of the "Jesus" Colton saw while "in heaven," it appears he likewise has been demonically deceived.

The connection between Colton's experience and that of Akiane Kramarik extends beyond this vision of "Jesus." Both of them describe heaven as a place replete with indescribable color. Interestingly, this is something common to the experience of many occultists who have "visited heaven" or have had a brush with death; "euphoria, music, and color surpassing anything known in the natural physical state" often describe the event.[5]

---

5 Marilyn Ferguson, *The Aquarian Conspiracy*, (New York: St. Martin's Press, 1980), 384.

Mr. Burpo also seems to accept an explanation of the Trinity based upon a child's song and (apparently) Mormon doctrine. When asked to describe God the Father, Colton says he is "really, really big" (page 100) so big he can hold the whole world in his hands. Colton goes on to say this physical God sits next to Jesus while nearby sits the Holy Spirit who is "kind of blue" (page 103). The Bible presents a different point of view.

According to the apostle John, *No man hath seen God at any time; the only begotten Son, which is in the bosom of the Father, he hath declared him* (John 1:18, cf. John 6:46, 1 John 4:12). This is so because God is *the King eternal, immortal, invisible* (1 Timothy 1:17) *who lives in unapproachable light, whom no one has seen or can see* (1 Timothy 6:16). Indeed, *no one may see [God] and live* (Exodus 33:20).

Furthermore, the description of the Trinity provided by Colton via Mr. Burpo has more in common with Mormon doctrine than orthodox Christianity. Members of the LDS organization believe God the Father is in the form of a man; the Eternal Son in his deity is likewise flesh and blood, and the Holy Spirit is "both a substance, a fluid, and a person"[6] (which sounds "kind of blue"). Hence, Mormons would have no problem with the description of the Trinity provided in *Heaven Is For Real*.

Mr. Burpo also receives Colton's fanciful recital of "the coming war" as gospel truth. The child claims he saw a future event wherein "there's going to be a war, and it's going to destroy this world. Jesus and the Angels and the good people are going to fight against Satan and the monsters and the bad people. I saw it." Colton goes on to say the battle is against literal dragons and monsters and is fought with swords and bows.

Apparently it escaped the notice of Mr. Burpo that Colton's statement on "the Battle of Armageddon" came some three years after his stay in the hospital and only after he had viewed the video presentation of *The Lion, The Witch And The Wardrobe*, replete with "fantasy/ medieval battle scenes," swords, armor and all sorts of monsters and other mythical creatures. Clearly, Colton's "memory" of that "heavenly vision" is tied directly to his viewing the video. It is mind boggling that anyone would base their

---

6 Walter Martin, *The Kingdom Of The Cults*, (Minneapolis: Bethany House Publishers, 1977), 178 – 184.

understanding of Scripture on this kind of foolishness.

In Revelation chapter 19, Christ is depicted as riding forth on a white horse (no mention of a rainbow pony) to strike the nations with the sword that proceeds from his mouth. This illustrates how "Christ destroys the evil nations not with a literal sharp sword but with the proclaimed word that comes out of his mouth (cf. 1:16; Isaiah 11:3-5). But what words come from the Messiah's mouth? The Christian proclamation of the slain lamb, who is named "Faithful and True" (cf. Ephesians 6:17). That is, by the preaching of the gospel about Christ's faithfulness to God, the claims of the anti-Christian kingdom and its rulers are exposed as lies and deceptions; and by its message, God's condemnation of the nations is found to be true (cf. Hebrews 4:11-12)."[7] There is nothing in the

---

7 Robert W Wall, *New International Biblical Commentary: Revelation*, (Peabody: Hendrickson Publishers, 1991), 232. Also H. B. Swete who says the passage exemplifies "the whole course of the expansion of Christianity: the conversion of the Empire; the conversion of the Western nations which rose on the ruins of the Empire; the conversion of the South and the far East, still working itself out in the history of our own time. In all St. John would have seen Christ using the Sword of His mouth; the white horse and his Rider, the diadem-crowned head, the invisible armies of heaven." H. B. Swete, *Commentary on Revelation* (Grand Rapids: Kregel Publications, [1911] 1977), p. 254.

Bible that should be interpreted as a "last battle" fought by men armed with actual swords against literal dragons and monsters.

Another feature of Colton's alleged celestial visit is that the entire episode lasted just three minutes even though Colton tells of happenings that would have taken hours or even days to occur. Mr. Burpo says this must indicate heavenly time is different from earthly time. However, there is no scriptural basis for this opinion. According to Scripture, time is part of the created realm and all of the universe – including heaven - is subject to it (Genesis 1:1, 14). God has accredited the ineradicable nature of time in the created realm by his use of it throughout history (Exodus 9:18, Deuteronomy 11:14, 2 Kings 4:16, Ecclesiastes 3:11, Acts 14:17 and so on). Indeed, the whole of Scripture presents reality as unfolding in lineal time. In other words, time in God's realm is movement from point A to point B along the continuum and is measured in recognizable increments. Truly, *this is what the LORD says, he who appoints the sun to shine by day, who decrees the moon and stars to shine by night, who stirs up the sea so that its waves roar— the LORD Almighty is his name: "Only if these decrees vanish from my sight," declares the LORD, "will the descendants of Israel ever cease to be a nation before me'* (Jeremiah 31:35-36, cf. Psalm 104:19-23). In short, day, night and the regular turning of the tide are evidence of God's trustworthiness. There is no biblical evidence he lays that consistency aside in heaven. Rather, God ever accommodates himself to "human time" even though he is not constrained by time (2 Peter 3:8).

On the other hand, "magical time" is "beyond time, independent of time"[8] and in the holographic mystical state "4000 years ago is the same as tomorrow."[9] And to the practiced sorcerer "one moment can be an eternity."[10]

Colton's claim that Jesus has a rainbow colored pony calls to mind "My Little Pony" and "Rainbow Brite" the little girl who can "bring sparkles of color to the darkest day and put a bright smile on little girls faces" who is often seen gliding "through the air on her magical flying horse, Starlight."[11] Although the rainbow is a sign of God's covenant promise to never again

---

8 North, 182
9 Ferguson, 184
10 North, 153
11 Phil Phillips, *Turmoil In The Toy Box*, (Lancaster: Starburst Publishers, 1986), 82.

destroy the Earth by flood (Genesis 9:13-16), New Agers and Neopagans, have given it a different meaning. To the New Age devotee, rainbows "represent a bridge between the individual and the Universal Mind, which, in the branch of the New Age which regards itself as esoteric Christianity, is referred to as Saint Kumara, one of the terms for Lucifer. In this context the rainbow is termed the Antahkaranah" the rainbow bridge between man and Lucifer who, they say, is the oversoul.[12] For this reason I am likewise uncomfortable with Colton's obsession with rainbows (page 107) following his out-of-body experience.[13]

Colton also claims that the angel Gabriel sits at the left hand of God's throne (page 101). According to the Bible, to sit at the left-hand or the right-hand of a person of authority is an honor. For instance, the mother of James and John asked Jesus to allow her sons to sit at the left and right hand of the Lord in his kingdom. But Jesus said, *to sit on my right hand and on My left is not Mine to give, but it is for those for whom it is prepared by My Father* (Matthew

---

12 Herbert J. Pollitt, *The Inter-Faith Movement: The New Age enters the Church*, (Carlise: The Banner Of Truth Trust, 1996), 164.
13 Akiane Kramarik also talks about seeing incredible rainbow colors in her visions of heaven.

20:23). To say the angel Gabriel sits at the left hand of the father is to ignore the fact we live in the age of the Son of Man.

The old covenant age was the age of angels. Angels led the people of God through the wilderness, went before them in battle and delivered the law to Moses (Acts 7:38, 53, Galatians 3:19, Hebrews 2:2). Indeed, in the old covenant era, Satan, a fallen angel, was allowed to stand in the presence of God and accuse the brethren (Job 1:6-12, Zechariah 3:1-2). With the coming of the new covenant age, the age of the Son of Man, Satan was cast out of heaven (Luke 10: 17-20, Revelation 12:9). We no longer have an accuser who stands before God but an advocate in Jesus Christ our Lord, the only mediator between God and man (1 Timothy 2:5).

Thus, angels do not occupy a place of special honor before God in the new covenant age. They no longer act as mediators for mankind. For these reasons it also would be impossible to see Satan while in heaven (page 134). To suggest otherwise is to return to the old covenant condition. Certainly, this is a circumstance the devil would like to see and there is no doubt he would like to confuse believers on this issue.

Finally, spiritism or consulting the dead is strictly prohibited by the Bible (Deuteronomy 18:11, cf. Leviticus 19:31, 20:6). Scripture does not detail the forbidden practice but simply says it is detestable to God.

Necromancers often attempt to contact the spirits of dead ancestors, seeking advice and protection for the living. It may seem cute to claim that a little boy was taken under the wing (excuse the pun) of his long dead great-grandfather in the hereafter but there is no such thing as "white magic necromancy" or "Christian consulting the dead." The practice is satanic under any circumstance.

Hence, there are no exclusions to the biblical injunction against necromancy. Nor is there any reason to believe that such communications with (pretended) departed spirits are less offensive to God now than in the time of Moses.

Furthermore, there is no exception made for someone who has a near death experience (or dies) and communicates with the dead while in the condition of near death or "dead" and returns to tell about it. Nor is an exception made for someone who supposedly "travels" to heaven in a vision and returns. Thus, Paul said nothing about speaking with departed saints.

John's account is related in highly symbolic terms and so we cannot consider his communication with the elders to be normative – or even an account of an actual communication with a departed saint. Moreover, the story of King Saul and the witch of Endor is instructive to us today as an example of a man who rebelled against God's revealed word but still sought the blessings of the Almighty. Frankly this is similar to the attitude of present day Christians who turn their back on Scripture in favor of extra biblical revelation.

In light of the clear commandments disallowing communication with the dead (with no provision for exceptions), we are obligated to reject *all* forms of necromancy out of hand. Thus, we must immediately reject the legitimacy of an alleged visit to heaven wherein interaction with departed saints is professed - no mater how prettily the picture is painted.

On the other hand, necromancy that has been "christianized" by a child's story of visiting heaven, meeting important Bible figures, staying at the "heavenly home" of a long departed great-grandfather and so on, is just the sort of thing the devil might use to force the nose of the occult camel under the church tent.

As in the case of the practical problems with the story, there are other items in the book that raise theological red flags (such as "power shot down from heaven" by the Holy Spirit, Colton's "sister" being anxious to see her parents in heaven etc.) but the issues already treated are adequate to show that *Heaven Is for Real* is theologically unsound.

· Four ·
The Primary Theological Problem

The fundamental problem with *Heaven Is For Real* is that it constitutes extra biblical revelation.

Extra biblical revelation is any kind of knowledge or experience that provides information concerning God, his work or his will, that is not drawn directly from Scripture. It is equivalent to saying "thus sayeth the Lord" and the implication is that the new information is gospel truth.

The writers of the heavenly holographs are telling us that the Bible is better understood in light of their special spiritual experiences. They are telling us that the Bible is inadequate and the past 2000 years of Christianity have been sub-par because no one knew Jesus has a rainbow colored horse. They tell us that their heavenly journey has finally put to rest certain pesky doctrinal disputes and revealed God's will as never before. In the book and in publicity interviews, Mr. Burpo gives every indication that he accepts Colton's story as unquestionably true. He claims to be delighted with the revelation that everyone in heaven is about 30 years old. He is satisfied that Colton's description of Jesus has settled the issue of Christ's physical appearance once and for all.

If we begin to accept extra biblical revelation we immediately find ourselves on a slippery slope. Where do we draw the line? At what point do we stop revising our doctrine to accommodate the new revelation? In truth, once we begin the process it is impossible to stop for there is always someone with a new "revelation" who believes *they* should have the final word. If we accept without any biblical warrant the idea that Jesus has a rainbow colored horse, on what grounds do we reject the claim from a similar source that Christ's mediation has been supplanted by "angelic" representation?[14] There

14 Kevin and Alex Mallarkey, *The boy who came back from heaven*, (Carol Stream: Tyndale House Publishers Inc., 2010, 2011), 186.

is no consistent cause for doing so.

This is the fundamental reason we must reject all revelatory experience as spurious; to accept the Burpo narrative is to violate the integrity of the biblical canon. If Colton really did go to heaven and speak directly to God then it is time to revise the Bible and bring it up to date, for the Burpo tale contradicts the Bible at many points. This is the real problem with every story of a trip to heaven; they demand to be placed on par with Scripture, indeed to supplant it. You can't have it both ways. Either God's word is our final authority and the Burpo story is false or the Burpo story is true and supersedes the Bible. For Bible believing Christians the answer is clear: we stand upon the absolute authority of God's written Word. Conflicting information must be rejected as originating in human imagination or satanic deceit. The irony is, those who demand a place for extra biblical revelation are the first to reject the biblical punishment for false prophets. Yet, it is their position on the issue that would require its unchanging application (Deuteronomy 13:1-4 etc.).

Make no mistake; if we accept or even tolerate their story we are guilty of the same rebellion as they. It is not revelatory experience but Scripture that *is God-breathed and is useful for teaching, rebuking, correcting and training in righteousness, so that the man of God may be thoroughly equipped for every good work* (2 Timothy 3:16-17). No personal spiritual experience is fresher or more intimate than Scripture. God doesn't need to give us private revelation to help us in our walk with him. If we ignore this fact we will be *tossed back and forth by the waves, and blown here and there by every wind of teaching and by the cunning and craftiness of men in their deceitful scheming* (Ephesians 4:14 NIV).

I am not saying the Holy Spirit no longer speaks to Christians; he most certainly does. But he speaks to us and directs us individually and always in agreement with the Bible. He no longer inspires individuals with the Word of God as a means of directing the lives of others.

The current ministry of the Holy Spirit does not add to the Bible nor constitute new revelation. We cannot develop or "enhance" Christian doctrine using extra biblical experience or a "word from the Lord" no matter how wonderful the story may be. God *has given to us all things that pertain to life and godliness, through the knowledge of Him who called us by glory and virtue* (2 Peter 1:3).

The Holy Spirit illuminates a man's mind so he may know Christ. The Spirit enables him to apply the Word to his own life and arena of activity and to mature in Christlikeness. *Mature* Christians are enabled to offer godly advice and instruction (1 Timothy 4:13, 5:17, Hebrews 13:7). But with the passing of the first century and the realization of the new covenant (1 Corinthians 13:10), no one is commissioned to disclose "new truth" by virtue of mystic experience. We have been given exactly what we need in the written Word, the ministry of teaching and the individual elucidation of the Holy Spirit (cf. Jeremiah 31:34, Hebrews 8:11).

The Burpos should have recounted Colton's story to a mature spiritual authority and asked for counsel but they should not have gone public with their tale. As the preceding pages of this booklet have shown, Bible based counsel would have quickly uncovered the ungodly nature of the narrative. This would have forestalled the damage that has been inflicted upon those who have been deceived by *Heaven Is For Real*.

· Five ·
Conclusion

In conclusion, *Heaven Is for Real* does not rise to a reasonable standard of credibility by any estimation. Mr. Burpo's explanation for his son's experience is unbelievable and the theology presented in the book is contrary to sound Bible doctrine. Furthermore, the message of the book serves to turn one's attention away from Jesus Christ and focus it upon experience and emotion. Rather than inspire readers to place faith in Jesus alone, it guides people to locate their source of encouragement outside a living relationship with Christ. People claim the book will: convince readers heaven exists, make "the future more hopeful," and "[reaffirm] how important faith is in our lives."[15]   Many of the

---

15 These words come from the endorsements found at the front of *Heaven Is For Real*.

reader reviews found online claim the Burpo tale has "renewed [their] faith in God and the afterlife in heaven." Yet, these blessings are to be sought in a relationship with Jesus Christ and in the study of Scripture not through extra biblical revelation.

Are we now so spiritually impoverished we must seek God "speaking to us in this twenty-first century through the unblemished eyes of a child"?[16] Unblemished? The Bible says otherwise: *Surely I was sinful at birth, sinful from the time my mother conceived me* (Psalms 51:5, NIV). It is derisory to believe a tall tale simply because it comes from a child. Foolishness is bound up in the heart of a child (Proverbs 22:15) and it is wrong to promote the cultivation of foolishness by encouraging this sort of imagina- tiveness. Moreover, Scripture tells us that childish leadership is a sign of God's displeasure. *I will give children to be their princes, and babes shall rule over them* (Isaiah 3:4) says God to unfaithful Israel. "This also was fully accomplished in the succession of weak and wicked princes, from the death of Josiah to the destruction of the city and temple, and the taking of Zedekiah, the last of them, by Nebuchadnezzar."[17] It is accomplished

---

16 Jo Anne Lyon, General Superintendent, The Wesleyan Church: found in the endorsements located at the front of *Heaven Is For Real*.

today in the church when Believers look to children for leadership and theological insight.

There are a number of explanations to choose from to explain Colton's visions. In the first place, the book may be nothing more than a presentation of a young boy's imaginative musings as encouraged by his gullible father. His original exclamation that angels sang to him while he was in the hospital certainly points that direction. It is just the sort of thing a four year old child born and raised in the church *would* say. The rest of the story could have been man-ufactured over the months and years as the child was prompted by his parents. The obvious connections to demonic deception may have been suggested by the enemy at the same time. In my opinion, this is the most likely scenario.

Another explanation may be that the entire account was made up by the parents and repeated to the Burpo child so frequently, he accepted it as his own experience. An additional sinister explanation would be that Colton fell under the influence of unclean spirits while sedated during surgery and Mr. Burpo failed to protect and correct his son. This is not to suggest Colton now or ever has been demon possessed but to say he may have been

---

17 Adam Clarke's *Commentary On The Bible*, Electronic Edition, Isaiah 3:4.

influenced by ideas planted in his mind by minions of the devil while in a vulnerable state. Yet it is really not for me to say what is behind the story. Obviously I don't know; I offer these explanations only to show there are possibilities other than the one proposed by the book.

Perhaps a more troubling issue is the theological illiteracy that has helped propel *Heaven Is For Real* to best seller status. Frankly this book project should have never gotten off the ground. In my view, Mr. Burpo's church and denomination should have counseled him to turn away from his error and levied sanctions in the circumstance of his refusal to do so.

The many Christians who have read and enjoyed *Heaven Is For Real* need to recognize their doctrinal ignorance and make an effort to correct the problem. They need to study God's word in depth on a daily basis and insist on solid Bible teaching from the pulpit. Until then books like *Heaven Is For Real* will continue to spread their malignant influence throughout the Body of Christ.

D. Eric Williams has ministered throughout the Mountain-West region of the United States since 1988. In addition to his current pastorate at Cottonwood Community Church in Cottonwood Idaho, he is the Chaplain at the Idaho state Veterans Home in Lewiston Idaho. He holds a BA from the University of the State of New York a MA from the Southern California Graduate School of Theology and is ordained with the Conservative Congregational Christian Conference. Eric, his wife, and nine children, and have home-schooled for more than 20 years.

Eric's ministry is focused on Christ centered expository Bible teaching that is covenantal in nature. His goal is to help families fulfill the kingdom mandate by developing a Christian worldview firmly founded on biblical truth. You may contact Eric at mail@dewms.com, or at P.O. Box 1037, Lewiston Idaho, 83501. Pastor Williams' personal web site is dewms.com. His books are featured at comwriter.com and other online booksellers.

Men Of Issachar

Understand The Times, Know What To Do
ISBN/EAN13: 1441435670 / 9781441435675
Page Count:190

According to Webster's dictionary a crisis  is a "decisive moment or an unstable or crucial time or state of affairs" in history. It is fashionable to suggest the early 21st century is a time of crisis. We are told by our leadership that crisis is at every hand. Indeed, when crisis does not materialize as quickly or as violently as one might expect it seems civil leadership is not averse to creating "crisis."

However, we are in the midst of crisis. The situation we face today is not economic, environmental, political or sociological. Instead, it is a crisis of leadership at the most elementary level. It is a crisis requiring a dramatic cultural shift in order to correct the course of history. As things now stand we are headed for disaster. Indeed, we are experiencing the slow unfolding of disaster all around us even today.

Real Faith

Studies In The Epistle Of James
ISBN/EAN13: 1441436782 / 9781441436788
Page Count: 174

The Epistle of James is all about Faith - real faith, living faith, active faith. Like the apostle Paul, James would have us work out our

salvation with fear and trembling. This book endeavors to show how that is done.

According to James' epistle, real faith is based upon certain presuppositions. True faith finds joy in hardship. Faith brings unity in the body; it engenders self control; it benefits the individual and the world at large.

Real Faith, Studies In The Epistle Of James will en-able you to read the letter of James with fresh eyes and allow you to apply this misunderstood book to your walk of faith.

I am happy to commend D. Eric Williams' studies in the epistle of James. "Real Faith" is down-to-earth, just like the epistle, and is well-suited to help the reader unpack the kind of practical help that James is known for. Douglas Wilson

The End Was Near

End Times Bible Prophecy
Made Simple
ISBN/EAN13: 1451591209 / 9781451591200
Page Count: 140

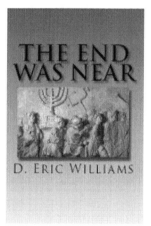

Are we living in the Last Days? Are the End Times upon us? Many popular writers confidently say we are the terminal generation - but is that what the Bible says? Find out in this introductory study of biblical eschatology by Pastor and writer D. Eric Williams.

In this brief overview of the topic, Pastor Williams reveals the proper approach to interpreting End Time passages and provides the tools necessary for understanding biblical eschatology.

Shine Forth As The Sun

The Messianic Reign In Parable
According To Matthew's Gospel
ISBN/EAN13: 144143772X / 9781441437723
Page Count: 225

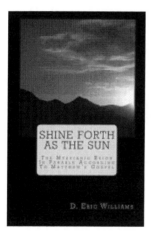

The kingdom of God: when will it begin? What are its characteristics? Who will be a part of it? Drawing from the "kingdom is like" parables of our Lord Jesus Christ, Pastor D. Eric Williams examines these questions and more in this collection of sermons concerning the kingdom of God according to Matthew's Gospel.

Also By D. Eric Williams

The Christmas Season
Stories For Each Week of Advent
And Christmas Eve
ISBN/EAN13: 1434816575 / 9781434816573
Page Count: 120

The Power Presentation
Career Acceleration Through Public Speaking
ISBN/EAN13: 1434818985 / 9781434818980
Page Count: 150

Quasimodo On Skis
A Collection Of Humorous Essays Designed to
Produce A Chuckle In Even The Most
Curmudgeonly Of People
ISBN /EAN 13: 1460931971 / 978-1460931974
Page Count: 101